love an alternative perspective

mad
moose
press

Managing Editors: Simon Melhuish and Emma Craven
Series Editor: Lee Linford
Contributors: Simon Melhuish, Emma Craven, Lee Linford, Nikole G. Bamford

Design: Alan Shiner
Illustrations: Justine Waldie
Photography: Getty Images

Designed and compiled by
Mad Moose Press
for
Lagoon Books
PO Box 311, KT2 5QW, UK
PO Box 990676, Boston, MA 02199, USA

ISBN: 1-904139-15-9

www.madmoosepress.com
www.lagoongames.com

Printed in China.

Love is a serious mental disease.
Plato

Love is a blind warfare.
Ovid

Love is all you need.
Paul McCartney

Need love? Who doesn't?

If you thought that love was confusing enough already then you were wrong. It's time to delve into matters of the heart and take a look through entirely different eyes. Forget Mars and Venus, this kind of love is way out there.

Prepare yourself for an unconventional visual journey through love's many minefields, punctuated with a few words of wisdom and some rather more conventional interpretations.

crush ▶ *verb* compress through forceful or violent pressure, so as to break, damage, injure or reshape; breakdown or grind into smaller particles or powder by exerting pressure; overwhelm or defeat forcibly. • *noun* a large group or crowd of people, typically within a confined space;

(slang) infatuation or intense feeling of desire, experienced over a short period of time;

a juice drink derived from pressed fruit.

blind date

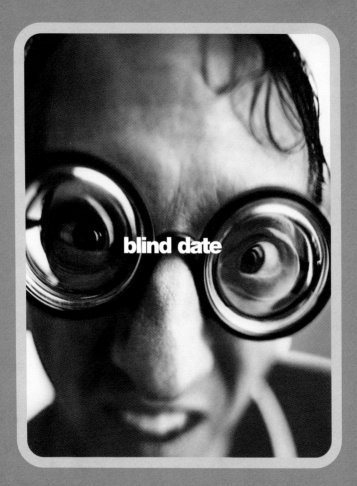

blind date

encounter

In everyone's life, at some time, our inner fire goes out. It is then burst into flame by an encounter with another human being. We should all be thankful for those people who rekindle the inner spirit.

Albert Schweitzer

first impressions

Love at first sight
is cured by
a second look.

Proverb

first impressions

attraction

intuition ▶ *noun* instantaneous insight or acquisition of the truth, without prior knowledge or reasoning: instinctive feeling or perception: *intuition told her that they would be together before the night was through.*

intuition

chemistry

First feelings are always the most natural.

Louis XIV

chemistry

connection

connection

feeling ▸ *noun* a physical sensation experienced through touch; emotional sensitivity or reaction. **feelings** emotional sensitivities or susceptibility esp. triggered by a reaction to an individual or situation.

feelings

desire

What the eye does not admire,
the heart does not desire.

Proverb

first move

first move

At the touch of love, everyone becomes a poet.

Plato

touched

hold ▶ *verb* grasp, retain or support in hands or arms; remain in possession of (property, estate, stocks etc.); maintain in a constant position (object, person etc.); contain or have the capacity to do so; embrace (a person) or support in arms; detain or restrain against free will, esp. by authority or in custody; sustain a course or line of progress in a specific direction.

kiss

caress

**Love may be blind,
but it can sure find its
way around in the dark!**

Anonymous

intimate ▶ *adjective* closely acquainted; having considerable familiarity (with something or someone); a cosy, friendly atmosphere in a conducive place or environment: indication of a sexual relationship or sexual involvement between two people; of a personal nature; *noun* a close friend.

intimate

rendezvous

rendezvous

Passion makes the
world go round.
Love just makes it
a safer place.

Ice-T

passion

affection ▶ *noun* warm, gentle sensation or feeling of fondness or love.

head over heels

**Love is swift of foot;
love's a man of war,
and can shoot,
and hit from far.**

George Herbert

idolize

It's not the beauty of a woman that blinds the man, the man blinds himself.

Proverb

idolize

obsession

obsession

tremble

Let men tremble to win the hand of woman, unless they win along with it the utmost passion of her heart.

Nathaniel Hawthorne

butterfly ▶ noun (*pl. -flies*) a winged insect, often brightly coloured, diurnal in nature; an unreliable, whimsical or irresponsible person. **butterflies** a fluttering sensation experienced in the stomach typically during times of nervousness or apprehension; a swimming stroke involving the action of lifting both arms simultaneously from the water and moving them forwards before re-entry.

romance

romance

together ▶ *adverb* in the company of another person or people; to act or be in conjunction or unison with something or someone;

close or intimate involvement of two people over a sustained period, through sexual relationship or marriage;

continuity in unbroken succession. *adjective* displaying rationality, practicality and confidence.

together

compatibility

When two partners are of one mind,
clay is into gold refined.

Proverb

compatibility

DO NOT
DISTURB

dirty weekend

involved

As for the lover, his soul dwells in the body of another.

Marcus Cato

involved

genuine ▶ *adjective* of authenticity and repute; not counterfeit, the real thing; pure-bred; sincerity of emotion or gesture esp. within a close relationship.

respect

Where we do not respect
we soon cease to love.

Proverb

tender ▶ *adjective* demonstrating gentleness, affection or love.

The easiest kind of relationship
for me is one with 10,000 people.
The hardest is with one.

Joan Baez

relationship

consideration ▶ *noun* contemplation or deliberated thought, often over a period preceding the making of a decision;

display of sensitivity, thoughtfulness or compassion towards the feelings of others;

make allowance or provision for when passing judgement or reaching a conclusion; fee or compensation made as a payment.

consideration

support

support

devotion

Who travels for love

finds a thousand miles

not longer than one.

Proverb

devotion

engagement ▶ *noun* promise or commitment to marry.

ring

commitment

A ruddy drop of manly blood the surging sea outweighs; the world uncertain comes and goes, the lover rooted stays.

Ralph Waldo Emerson

commitment

trust

Mistrust is an axe in the tree of love.

Proverb

union ▸ *noun* connect or bring together to make one: political coalition or co-operation to form a singular or united state;

the harmonious joining together of two people in matrimony or marriage;

a group of employees assembled to defend their common interests: trade union; an organisation, club or body formed by a group of people with similar pastimes or interests.

marriage

share ▸ *noun* comparatively small allocation, piece or quota from a larger quantity, either contributed by or split between a group of people; a single unit of divisible equal parts representing a company's capital value; joint ownership of property; allocation of duties, tasks or responsibilities amongst a group of people expected to complete them: *verb* benefit or experience jointly with another or others, through relationship or mutual involvement.

share

partner

It takes two to Tango.

Proverb

eternity

Love is a symbol of eternity. It wipes out all sense of time, destroying all memory of a beginning and all fear of an end.

Anne Louise Germaine de Staël

eternity

Look out for the other titles in the Thought Provokers range:

Thought Provokers - LIFE
Thought Provokers - SPORT